David

A Mug of My Own

Prayers for the working day
and other aspects of adult life

kevin
mayhew

Also by David Gatward
published by Kevin Mayhew

Adverts and Advent
Can We Talk, Lord?
E-male
It's a Love Thing
It's Me Again, Lord
Leap Into Lent
Looking out the Window
Monday Mornings and Traffic Jams
Nite-nite Jesus
Time Out

First published in 2005 by
KEVIN MAYHEW LTD
Buxhall
Stowmarket
Suffolk 1P14 3BW

www.kevinmayhew.com

9 8 7 6 5 4 3 2 1 0

ISBN 1 84417 388 7
Catalogue No 1500791

Front cover by Jonathan Stroulger
Typesetting by Richard Weaver
Printed and bound in Great Britain

CONTENTS

ACKNOWLEDGEMENTS

The Gatward Clan – You're in every book for one simple reason: I think you're brilliant.

Penny – For giving me the opportunity to claim that my first house out of college was a mansion with a private swimming pool!

Ben – For the endless discussions, olives and wine, and, of course, the 'station of play'!

*For Dan, Abbi, Lex and the rest of the Bury Crew;
it's been a while now, but cheers for making my first
job and post-college life so utterly memorable.*

INTRODUCTION

Date: April 2005
Age: 32

This is a bit of a blast from the past: a book found in a dusty box in a cupboard while moving house! I actually wrote these prayers seven years ago, back when I first entered the workplace. In some ways it seems like yesterday, in others, like another life. I'm older now (though perhaps no more mature!) and my life is radically different. I live in another part of the country, work for a different employer, but deep down, I'm still me. How frightening!

Every stage in life presents new experiences, new decisions to be made, new rules to be followed or broken, and new mistakes to be made and learned from. And through it all is God's guiding hand. For that reason, I've left these prayers as I wrote them seven years ago. They're what I was going through at the time, so why change them and adjust them to where I am now? So I'll hand you over to the me of yesterday, a long-haired twenty-something, who's just left college and started his first job. . .

Date: April 1998
Age: 25

The work place – am I really here? is this really happening? (Yes, sorry Dave, but this is it . . . for the next 40 years.) Hard to believe really, but it's true. I've done the education thing; now it's time for the working thing; that wonderful world of fax machines and telephones, grown-ups, espresso and weekends away. And I'm still the same old me! That's the strange bit: I'm still the same old me. OK, I am different, but I'm still me. I remember when I was younger thinking that when I was older I'd feel different. Well, I don't.

One thing that has struck me is how much my childhood memories have featured in these new experiences. When you're young, everything is new, everything is something to touch, or taste or break; everything is there to be discovered. Starting your first job 'in the real world' is a bit like that experience of years ago. Only now if you break things or knock things over you have to pay for it, and if you do something stupid or daft you get called childish . . . as if it's supposed to be an insult!

Some people find it hard to deal with those of us who accept that we are not perfect and are very open about the mistakes we are always making. I find this amazing. I have a life ahead of me. I do not know how long it will be, but I know that I have a lot to learn and that I am always learning. I have guidelines and ideas and moral standards, but I also have a brain that questions, that thinks and likes to explore. I do things that I regret, I do things I'm not sure about, I do things I love (for whatever reason), and I do things for the sheer thrill. That is who I am, and this year has given me a huge number of things to deal with, as anyone who is at this stage of their life will understand.

And I am still here, and I still sit with God and laugh and cry and discuss. I talk things through, I disagree, I discover, I walk away, I come back. That is who I am: someone who is extremely lucky but still dissatisfied; who has been given a lot and still wants more; someone who has done things some people never will and still isn't happy; someone who is going through it all with God . . . and there lies the difference.

Being a Christian is about accepting who you are, where you are at, and believing with all that you are that God loves you and holds you close. Yes, you have to accept the right and the wrong in your life, but God doesn't expect change overnight. Peter hung out with Jesus for three years and still messed it up, and he's the rock that God built his Church upon! Now, what does that tell you? Exactly – God knows what we are like, loves us and laughs with us! Whether at work or play, old or young, at school or starting our first job, God loves us as we are (although he's big on changing you for the better) and he wants to be involved in everything we are and whatever we do. So, next time you're bored at work, send a fax to God . . . it would be just like the Omnipotent to reply!

David Gatward

GRADUATION DAY

This is it, Lord.
I did it.
Four years down the road,
   and here I am:
   about to walk on to a stage,
   shake the hand of royalty
   and then leave . . .

   a 'Graduate'.

Me, a graduate.
How?
This surely can't be possible.
After all those mess-ups with my A levels,
   a year out to 'think'
   (even though you and I would probably use the words
   'run away').
I don't feel ready.

I'm not ready.

Aren't I supposed to feel a little different?
Surely I should at least feel that I am an adult.
A grown-up.
Someone with direction, ambition,
   a yearning to go somewhere.

I don't, Lord.
I do not feel 'different'.
I feel scared.

This all used to seem so far away.
When I was younger,
   when all that was important
   was going down to the local river
   to catch minnows with my brother;
   or try to do a bunny hop on my BMX,
   or even stay out till dark on the swings
   down at the playground with a few friends.

It was a long way away,
   wasn't it, Lord?
I know because I can remember.
But why has it gone so quickly?
Why wasn't I allowed more time to go paddling,
   catapult shooting and sledging?
Why were the years of innocence and discovery
   so short lived?
Why did I have to grow up?

The thing that frightens me, Lord,
   isn't so much that all of it
   seems like yesterday,
   but that in fifteen years' time
   all this will seem just like yesterday:
Today,
   what I am doing and have done –
   my time at college,
   my friends,
   my old cottage near the pub that was home
   to 'the Brow Boys' for two years;
   my thoughts,
   my actions,
   my views –
   will all be a memory
   when I am
   what I'm still to become.

So, Lord, the me of today
   has a wish for the me of tomorrow.
As I step on to this platform,
   to shake the hand of my future
   and wave goodbye to my past,

   let these memories
   be as much a part of me then
   as they are now.

Amen.

ARRIVAL

I'm here, Lord –
   at the door to the office.
Inside lies a new part of my life,
   a part full of things to be discovered, explored,
   costed out and projected
   as future plans and estimations
   of yearly income.

Mmmmm . . .

My mind is full of questions
   and confusions
   and fear.
I do not know where any of this will lead.
I do not know if it is what I want to do.
I do not know if I've actually remembered
   to pack my sandwiches.
But I do know that I must take this first step,
   and that this will not be the first and last time
   that such a step will need to be taken.

So, Lord,
   this is it.
One more step
   and I'm off.

Watch over me, Lord.

Amen.

A MUG OF MY OWN

Lord,
   it's ten to nine,
   and I am now standing here
   waiting for the kettle to boil
   so that I can get my first caffeine kick of the day.

And here in my hand is the proof
   that all of this is for real.

A mug of my own.

I no longer use the spares,
   or the chipped ones.
I have reached that station in life which requires one
   to bring in a mug for the never-ending fountain of coffee.

And this mug,
   it is a great thing.
It is a sign of individuality.
It is a symbol of acceptance,
   and it is physical proof that I am here.

Here, Lord,
   where mornings mean getting up.

Where dinners remind me all too much
   of my packed lunches at primary school.
Where home time is even more valuable
   than I ever thought it could be.
And where holidays no longer mean weeks and weeks
   of nothing but den-building . . .
   and perhaps a little more den-building.

This mug is more important and significant
   than anything I have ever held in my hands.
It is only a cheap mug
   which can get chipped and not upset me.
It is nothing to look at,
   and could very easily be replaced.
But it is important.

I use it every day.
It helps to refresh me,
   to keep me awake,
   to warm me
   and to remind me
   that I am really here,
   that I have a job,
   and that I am doing something with my life.

Lord,
   as I stand here waiting to fill my mug,
   I give to you all that I am in this job.

From the enthusiastic, ideas-packed dynamo
   (which I am convinced exists in here, somewhere)
   to the caffeine-drugged,
   continuously worried
   and psychotically paranoid bloke
   (who I wish existed somewhere else).

As this mug is mine, Lord,
   waiting to be filled,
   so I am yours.

Your very own,
   self-confessed,
   slightly weird
   mug.

Lord, fill me.

Amen.

PACKING UP TO GO

That's it. I've had enough.
Sorry, Lord,
   but this box
   and that pile of clothes
   can take themselves outside
   and get shoved up the proverbial
   of the next stage of my life.

I am sick and tired
   of moving.

Every two or three months
   everything I have
   is once again thrown into boxes
   nicked from the local supermarket,
   shoved in the back of the car
   and driven somewhere else.
I see some people with only a few suitcases.
Perhaps a nice small box for essentials and nothing else.

So what is all this stuff?
Do those others have nothing,
   or do I have a blessed gift
   to acquire utter rubbish wherever I go?

All this stuff!
Just look at it!
I am sure I need it
   because I sorted through it all last week
   and threw out bag after bag of rubbish.
But,
   against all the odds,
   I still have this –
My answer to global stupidity.

Forget the food mountain,
   the milk mountain
   and the butter mountain.

Here for all to see
   is . . .
   the 'stuff mountain'.

And believe me, Lord,
   you won't get better stuff anywhere else.
This is quality.
Guaranteed to take up space,
   get on your nerves,
   be absolutely essential yet no use whatsoever.

Brilliant, eh?

No, not really. Not at all.
Because the reason this pile is so big,
   the reason there is so much stuff,
   is that I am clinging to it.

I am moving to a new area,
   a new house and new housemates.
Everything will be unfamiliar:
   the job,
   people,
   landscape,
   smell of home,
   feel of bed.

All unlike anything I have known.

I don't mean to hoard, Lord.
I don't mean to cling like a child
   to a comforting toy,
   but I need it.

I know my family are just a phone call away.
I know that I will make friends.
I know I'll be all right.
But I need something tangible, even if it is rubbish.

These things that lie before me,
    unyielding as I try to fit them in these boxes,
    are a part of me at the moment.
I need to take that part of me where I am going.

I will change;
    I know that, Lord.
The only way to allow something to grow
    is to prune it.
But you don't cut off all its branches straightaway
    and expect it to flourish.

It takes time.
I know that this stuff will be discarded as I grow,
    but at this moment it is important.

So, Lord,
    as this final box overflows
    with more of my essential rubbish,
    as I pack these boxes into my car
    and ready myself to go,
    help me learn to hang on to what I need
    and leave behind the things I don't.

Amen.

LORD, THIS AIN'T EASY

Lord,
  this ain't easy.
I knew the going might be tough –
  moving away,
  starting afresh.
New job, new place, new people – new life.
But there's even more to it than I thought.

New doesn't necessarily mean great,
  or nice, or friendly,
  or what I'm ready for.
Because, Lord,
  I'm not ready for this.

All those old feelings – I still have them.
All that confusion,
  that lack of direction, that uncertainty –
  it's all still here, inside me.

What am I doing?
None of this feels right, and I don't know why.
Will I always be like this?
Someone who spends every day of his life
  feeling unsure about the future,
  dissatisfied with the present,
  and missing the past.

The odd thing is,
  although the past was great,
  I'm very good at forgetting the bad bits,
  the hurt of growing.

And the growing pains still exist.

I'm at a stage now
  which I never believed I'd reach.
A real (better) job
  in the real world
  and all my closest friends
  miles away.

I used to hate phones
  but now they are a lifeline.
Is this what growing up is all about?
Is this what 'upwardly mobile' is?
Well, if it is,
  I don't like it.

I'm stuck on my own,
  in a strange part of the country,
  trying to get rid of my debts
  and wondering where I go next.

It's crazy really;
  because I've only been here for six months,
  but I sit here thinking to myself,
  'Well, which job next, Dave?
  You don't want to get trapped,
  you need to move up,
  move on,
  move out.'

But I want –
  no, I *need* –
  to be happy here and now
  with what I am, what I have
  and with where I'm heading.

Last year I was banging my head on the wall,
  screaming for direction,

for a purpose
for a little bit of progress.
Now, here I am further down the line,
    luckier than many,
    and still insecure.

Did you ever feel this way, Lord?
I wish I could reach out and touch you.
I speak to my friends on the phone
    and although they are there,
    I'd rather see them
    or give them a hug
    (in a blokish, manly sort of way, of course).
And I feel the same with you.

I sit here,
    day after day
    and chat to you,
    tell you what's going on,
    ask your advice
    but, Lord,
    I would give anything if this minute,
    right now,
    I could just reach out and hug you.
Just to feel your arms keeping me safe.
Just to know, physically, that you are by me.

I miss everyone, Lord,
    and even though I know they are there
    I miss the tangible evidence.

Hold me, Lord:
    don't let me go.

Amen.

WHAT AM I DOING?

Lord,
    what am I doing?

For some reason
    I have turned up at this 'party'
    knowing only one person,
    and that person is going to spend most of the night
    at the keyboard with the band.

Great.

An entire evening
    with a bunch of people I don't know,
    who didn't know I was coming here
    and are probably not that interested.

I must be mad.

Actually,
    I know I am.
I've been sitting here on my own,
    drinking this pint of slightly warm beer
    (southerners have absolutely no idea
    about how to brew beer, Lord)
    and no one has turned up yet.

Yippee.
I can hardly stand the excitement.
It is too much.
So much so, that I must sit down
    and have a drink.

Oh, look –
    I'm doing that already.
How fascinating.
A promising beginning
    to a great night of entertainment.

No, Lord,
    I am not happy.
Making friends was never this difficult.
Well, not quite.
A few parties,
    lots of people not knowing anyone
    and suddenly there you were –
    mates everywhere.

Now it is down to me,
    and a little courage.

It is so different now.
I am not nineteen
    with four years of college ahead of me.
I am twenty-three
    with a career.

Do you know, Lord,
    that I am now classed as an executive?
Now really!
Me!
Who is kidding whom?
I am very gifted in dreaming.
I have a huge talent for running away.
I am extraordinarily good
    at getting bored and restless.
But an executive?
Please!

Now don't get me wrong:
   I am happy.

I am happy
   and confused.
   (As you can see,
   I don't really change much, do I?)
   I am now in an adult world
   full of adult responsibility
   and other adults.
Not only do I now have to mix with them,
   I am one of them!
THEM!
The crushers of teenage freedom!
The holders of the keys!
The infinitesimally small-minded individuals,
   interested only in money and personal gain,
   and ignorant of the needs of this generation X!

How can this be?
How can it?

And still no one has turned up.
No one.
So here I sit,
   alone at this table,
   pint in one hand,
   thoughts of my future in the other.

I come once again, Lord,
   to your table.
I miss everything that has gone
   and been replaced by all of this.
I miss my friends,
   my family.

I miss the ease of going out for a chat.
I miss the fun of pretending to be a tourist
  and buying souvenirs.
I miss walking to Ambleside park at 12.30 am
  and discussing you in the children's fort
  until 3 am in the morning
  with two other bleary eyed,
  mumbling, freezing idiots.
I miss moving the huge public seat
  to the middle of the pavement
  near the White Lion pub
  because it seemed 'really funny' to do it.

I miss it all.
And now I am at the beginning of something else.
Another start
  to another race
  that has no winner.

Help me get to the finishing line, Lord.

Amen.

TO RENT OR NOT TO RENT

Lord,
   I've got itchy feet,
   and it has nothing to do
   with wearing trainers every day
   and not using some 'new and improved' foot powder.

Nope, nothing that simple.

Actually,
   it's downright irritating.
I've only been here a few months,
   and I am already bored with where I live.

It's not the job,
   but this house.
Living with someone else can get a little annoying.
Especially when I've had a hard day
   and all I want to do is come in,
   slob out
   and drink a really cold
   (and horribly cheap)
   bottle of lager.

I'm not denying the fact
   that I'm lucky to have somewhere to live.
Just that I've always lived with people,
   and I wouldn't mind some space of my own.

But herein lies a big decision.
Do I go ahead and rent another place,
   or do I do the dreaded deed,
   and buy a house?

I was always the one at college
   who was convinced
   that doing something like that was crazy.
After all,
   how do I know where I'll be in a year or so?
I might have to move because my job fell through
   or maybe I had to move up and out.
(Yeah, right.)

But here I am,
   a year or so into my working life,
   and already I am considering buying a house!
Talk about a change!

And what is even more bizarre
   is that it now seems like a good idea!

You know, Lord,
   I am even beginning to want to have my own garden –
   a little bit of land that I can cultivate how I see fit
   and spend summer evenings in.
Perhaps even a veg patch.

This really is all a bit fast,
   but I am almost enjoying it!
Rather than still feeling like a teenager
   and not wanting to grow up,
   I now feel like a teenager
   who can get a brand-new place of his own
   to do daft things to!

It's the ultimate bedroom that beckons!

Loads of rooms,
   me,
   my creativity (ish)
   and
   NO PARENTS!
Wahey!

Lord,
   if I make this next decision,
   if I take the next step
   to wherever it is I am going,
   make sure that when I open the door
   you'll be with me
   on the other side.

Amen.

MY OFFICE

I remember
   when I first moved into a bedroom of my own.
I was so chuffed!
My own space
   that didn't have to be shared
   with one of two brothers.
An area that I could call my own,
   fill with my own things
   and build dens in.
I even had it decorated the way I wanted:
   red, white and black striped wall paper,
   red and white striped carpet
   and red and white striped curtains.
It was totally cool!

Now I have an office of my own.
Well, not so much an office as a separate space.
A separate space
   to hold my computer.

Yes, Lord: my computer!
A computer for me to sit at
   and type letters to people.
There's even a diary for the year ahead.

This really is strange.

I have now been employed for some time.
I earn money
   (which should just about clear my overdraft by 2010):
   I have responsibility.

Oh dear.

Responsibility.
That's waking up in the morning
   with important things to do.
That's having to be organised.
That's having to prove myself to the company.
That's being allowed to use a fax machine on my own
   without having to ask or give a reason.

Oh dear, indeed.

I never thought I'd have my own office –
   well, I don't really
   because I share it with my boss –
   but let's just pretend for a moment;
   I need humouring!
All these new toys to play with:
   headed writing paper,
   a laser printer,
   a hole punch and about a million
   of those little yellow sticky notelets.

What I'm supposed to do with it all
   is another thing completely
   but I'll probably know all about that later on.

So there you go, Lord –
   my office at my new job.

And,
   as I sit here and contemplate what it all means –
   what I am supposed to be doing,
   and where on earth I've left my lunch –
   I come to you, Lord, to ask one small thing.

Sit by me.

Amen.

THE NEW FLAT

Well, Lord,
    what do you think?
Not bad, is it?
I know I haven't unpacked totally yet,
    but it looks OK, doesn't it?

This is my new flat,
    my new home –
    a place for me to live in
    and slob out in.

This is such a milestone in my life.
Previous places were shared with family,
    then friends,
    but this is mine.

All mine.

Look, my own bathroom!
Absolutely no chance of being interrupted,
    burst in upon,
    talked to
    or annoyed.
I will be able to relax in my own bath
    without coming across someone else's hair.
I will be able to take as long as I want reading my book
    on my loo.
(And if I happen to leave the toilet seat up,
    no one is going to complain!)

Excellent!

I even have my own kitchen,
    bedroom,
    front room
    and hallway!

My own kitchen
    which will not greet me in the morning
    with the leaning tower of last night's
    'Just thought I'd invite a few friends
    around for a bite to eat' party,
    but which I wasn't a part of.
A fridge with my own food,
    cupboards with my own plates and bowls.

And a front room to sit in, undisturbed,
    doing what I want to do,
    not having to enter into conversation
    or argument with anyone
    except me.

Except me?

Lord, this doesn't seem so great any more.
I know I've been looking forward to this for years.

At last a place for little old me.
But I have a nagging feeling inside
    that I'm going to miss a few things . . .

Baths without disturbances,
    without the uninvited appearance
    of most members of my family
    who decide that a person in a bath
    is a captive audience,
    someone in need of that old gag,
    'Don't mind if I go to the toilet, do you?'

Kitchens with shared washing-up.
Breakfasts with friends
   who have just nipped to the little butcher's
   for a few rashers of bacon,
   some black pudding
   and a few eggs
   for a mid-week cooked breakfast.

A fridge that at the beginning of the week
   was a site of religious ceremony
   as three hungry blokes looked upon its wonders
   and dreamed of the feasts that would be a part of their lives.

A front room that was rarely empty.
Music in the background
   (if you were a couple of hundred yards away).
Cups of tea and fresh coffee shared.
A Scalextric track, some guitars,
   a cigar butt or two,
   and a really strange video collection.
(Plus, of course, the occasional girl or two,
   'who I'm not interested in because she's spoken for
   and I've too much work to do –
   honest, no, really I have!')

I'm even going to have to do the shopping on my own.
No longer will three hunger-crazed individuals
   run riot around the huge Morrisons in Kendal,
   buying eight of everything,
   something to eat on the way home,
   three Kinder eggs,
   packets of tea with the best free gift,
   a lot of beer,
   and some pickled eggs . . .

This place of my own,
  with all its benefits
  and bonuses,
  has its low points too.

Each room reminds me
  of the fun I had when it wasn't just me.
When each room wasn't just mine
  but shared.

When privacy was there if you wanted it,
  but didn't outstay its welcome.

This place of my own, Lord,
  is a little scary now.
Not as exciting as it was.
Not as much fun.
But it is here that I must stay –
  accepting now and leaving 'then' behind.

So, as I make my first cup of tea
  in my new kitchen
  in this new area,

  stay close, Lord,
  and be the unexpected guest.

Amen.

FOR THE CHANGES

Lord,
  that was Mum!

I know you know,
  but I just thought I'd tell you!
She rang to see how I was.
Just to have a chat,
  tell me what was happening at home,
  how everyone is
  and what she was cooking for dinner.

It was great, Lord!

What is strange, though,
  is that even though I love my parents so much,
  I am so pleased that I don't live with them any more!
And I am quite sure that their opinion of this
  is slightly more animated than mine!
After all,
  they have finally got rid of the awkward son
  who didn't know what to do with his life,
  who got depressed,
  played the drums,
  hated academic work
  and lived in the land of dreams!

That son hasn't changed too much,
  has he, Lord?
I'm still that same annoying teenager
  who has so many dreams.

And I am still that son
   who has the same wonderful parents.

Thanks, Lord,
   for the changes
   that haven't happened.

Amen.

AMBITION

Lord?
Is it wrong to be really ambitious?
To really want to do something with my life,
    to succeed,
    climb up the ladder,
    and really achieve in my career?

It strikes me as slightly selfish,
    now and again as I sit at work,
    lucky to have a job,
    that inside there is a burning
    to go further still,
    and get better.

It drives me barmy, a lot of the time.
Rather than concentrating on what I am doing
    and where I am,
    I get wrapped up in what I want to do
    and where I want to be!

It's a little bit annoying, really.
I doubt that I'm the only person who thinks like this.
Just take a look at all the people my age who work in the city,
    driving themselves into oblivion
    as their job takes over,
    and the pounds in the bank
    increase by the month.

In some ways,
    my ambition comes from being slightly envious
    of those who are doing so well
    and getting themselves financially secure so soon.

It doesn't make me exactly happy, Lord,
    but I can't help it.
I want to do so well
    because I am conscious of the life that I have
    and how lucky I am to be given this gift.

I want to make the most of all that I have,
    and live my life to the best of my abilities,
    because I am so glad to be alive!

To live, to breathe!
To touch and feel,
    to experience and learn.

There is so much out there that I want to do,
    yet I know that I will not do it all.
There is no way I will ever achieve
    all the dreams that take flight in my mind.

But, Lord, there is one thought
    which I always keep close by me.
It's a bit of a cliché, I suppose,
    but the thought of reaching the end of my life
    and realising that I have not lived
    is the one thought that I refuse to have
    when I finally cross that line
    and speak to you face to face.

So, Lord,
    help me turn this ambition
    into a healthy appetite for life,
    so that the reason I want to do so much
    is not to acquire possessions,
    or be looked up to,
    or run a huge company,
    (although that would all be nice, Lord)

but simply to have lived my life
to the best of my abilities,
and squeezed everything I could
out of the greatest gift you have given me:

life.

Amen.

OH NO . . .

Lord,
   what have I done?
How has this happened?
I'm sure I did everything correctly.
I'm sure that everything was checked,
   read through,
   examined.

But obviously not.

Lord,
   I have, to put it bluntly
   (and you are my best friend
   so there is little point in trying to censor this),
   cocked it up.

What a total mess.
I feel terrible.
I've let myself down,
   and, more importantly,
   everyone else as well.
My mistake –
   my own negligence –
   has cost the company in time
   and money.

I can't even bear
   to look anyone in the face.
Especially my boss.
I've let her down too.

Everything was going so well,
   things were really coming on,
   and now I feel totally shot down.
My confidence in my work has vanished.
   I am quite sure that a lot of people here
   are not so much surprised
   as angry with me.

I really didn't mean to do it.
I really thought I had done everything.
There is no point lying
   (least of all to you),
   or even pretending
   that I thought I had done everything.
I really believed that I had.

Back then, that is.
But now, looking back,
   I know the mistakes.
How could I have been so stupid?
Well, there goes any chance of a rise.
There goes all chances of increased responsibility.
There goes my life.
Nice knowing you, son,
   but I guess that's it.
Down the drain,
   washed away.

Lord,
   what am I doing?
You got me here!
I'm sure you did.
After all, if I look back and try to see a path,
   the only route I can see
   is one you helped me find.
So it's your fault.

At least,
  I wish it was.
But then,
  if it was your fault
  you'd have put me here
  and taken away everything
  that makes me what I am,
  what you created me to be.

A free person.
And if I am to be free,
  I must be free to experience the good and the bad,
  the ups and the downs,
  the mistakes.
I'm sorry, Lord.
I just wish I hadn't made this mistake.
I want everything to go so well.
To show everyone that I'm not useless,
  but that I am capable.

Capable of doing what is right.
Capable of doing the job properly.
And capable of admitting my mistakes
  and getting on with the job in hand.

Lord, give me courage.

Amen.

'IF ONLY'S . . .

I am tired, Lord,
    of a particular phrase.
It seems to surface at some point every day.
It is not constructive,
    or useful,
    or necessary.

When I use it I often find
    that I end up peering into space
    and getting depressed a little.
All other thoughts which are of use are discarded,
    and my mind becomes full
    with an eternal list of 'if only's
    which have been carefully collected
    over the years of my life.

The 'if only's, Lord.
The things I should have done but didn't.
The things which, when looked back on,
    would have been so different
    had I done this or that.
Things I never did
    but wish I had.

And so it is that I spend far too long
    wasting my time thinking
    about what I could have done,
    and end up regretting
    all that I did.

Not constructive, not necessary.
But something which occupies my mind far too much.

I don't mean to do it.
I don't *want* to do it.
But my fixation with self-pity
    leads me to those same issues
    time and again
    as I begin to believe
    that my life has been made up
    of one wrong decision
    after another.

What annoys me most of all is that these 'if only's
    are not about really important issues.
They are not to do with things
    which greatly affected the course of my life,
    but about small things –
    spur-of-the-moment decisions
    which at the time
    were the only things I could do or say.
And I regret them, Lord.

But then I start to imagine
    what could have happened.
What would have happened *if* . . .

If I had not said this and that,
    then perhaps that wouldn't have happened,
    but this would have.
If I had decided to go here instead of there,
    then this might have happened.

It's torture, Lord,
    and I do it willingly –
    no one makes me.
I do it to myself so I am to blame.

The trouble with looking back and saying 'if only'
   is that I look back with what I know now
   and forget what I knew then.
The things I did and the decisions I made
   were the best I could do at the time.
I often knew no better
   or had no choice.
I'm not saying that the things I did
   were always right,
     just that I did what I did
   and that's all there is to it.

I can't go back and change what has happened.
All I can do is learn from my mistakes
   and not do the same next time round.

Perhaps it is here
   that I see a point to the things I have done,
   the life I have lived.
Looking back at the 'if only's
   is a pointless exercise
   if all I do is wallow in what I could have done.
Yet, if I look back
   and learn from what I have done
   then there is a purpose.

I must learn not to throw away
   the things which I have done;
   the things which I may or may not regret,
   but instead, look at them and learn from them.
Turn the 'if only's in to
   'this time I'll learn from my mistakes';
   instead of regretting the things I have done
   accept that they all form a part of what I am –
   the person you created and love.

Lord,
    as the ifs and the buts of my life find me,
    help me not to run away,
    or waste my time wishing
    I'd done something I didn't do.
Help me to learn from my mistakes
    and grow.

Amen.

DEBT

Lord,
   I am worried.
No, don't put your head in your hands
   and weep because I'm off again!
I really am worried.

You see, I now have a mortgage,
   a car,
   lots of bills
   and still a huge amount of student debt –
Thousands of us leave college with a penalty
   for having gone to further our education.
Odd, really.

It's as if the country has turned round
   and told those of us
   who managed to get to college
   that we didn't actually go up a ladder on the board,
   but slipped down a snake
   and are actually worse off for it.

Why is this, Lord?
Do you understand?
After all,
   so many people expect you to understand things,
   that I just can't see how it is possible for you
   to understand every little problem.

What bothers me, Lord,
   is that this country of ours
   is turning to its people

and penalising them for something
that they should not be penalised for.

The only physical way for me to clear this debt
    is to suddenly land a job
    that pays twice what I earn at the moment.
Then, at least,
    I would be able to pay the whole lot off
    and feel a little more secure.
But I don't.

I don't have an answer to this, Lord,
    and I'm not expecting one from you.
Neither am I expecting a ridiculous pay rise,
    or a sudden generous donation.
All I need, Lord,
    is a little bit of patience.

This world is hardly perfect,
    and it seems to make sense
    that I should feel some contempt
    for a world being built upon the belief
    that those at the top
    should do better and better
    whilst those less fortunate
    should keep getting kicked,
    even if they manage to do something with their lives.

But this contempt is not unhealthy, Lord,
    and I pray you help me keep it.
Because it is this contempt
    that will keep me on the right track.
It is this distaste for unfairness
    that will make sure

that if I ever do well,
and find myself at the top,
I'll never forget being a little lower down.
And I pray, Lord,
    that this knowledge will allow me
    to make a few changes where I can
    to help those who will probably face
    even greater problems
    than I ever thought existed.

Lord, help me build on this.
Let this hatred of injustice
    become a weapon
    so that I can stand with those who fight
    and make a difference.

Lord,
    arm me.

Amen.

A LITTLE PATCH OF GREEN

Lord,
   I'm sitting in this garden of mine,
   the one I got with the house
   which I bought,
   even though six months ago
   I never thought I actually would.
And it's great!

Boy, am I lucky!
OK, so I'm not in London
   earning twenty-five grand
   and living it up.
But I do have this –

   a little patch of green.

A little bit of 'Olde England'
   that I can dig in,
   plant in
   and grow my own food in.

It's a lovely summer evening at the moment.
Everything is quiet,
   and I'm out here on one of the deck chairs
   Mum and Dad left me,
   on my own patio,
   near my own shed,
   outside my own kitchen window.
I've a little bit of jazz on in the background
   (Thelonious really hits it right!)
   and this glass of red is just perfik.

Lord,
   I thank you.
I know that to so many
   I have been a bit of a git these last few weeks.
Believe me I've got right on my nerves –
   always complaining,
   whingeing,
     moping around.

I just wasn't settled.
I had nowhere to put down some roots.

Until now.

In this little piece of heaven
   that I now call home.
And this really does feel like home.
After all,
   everything I own
   now resides under one roof,
   and that roof belongs to me!

Now that is something!

Settling down isn't so bad, after all.
Knowing that all this is my own.
That all I have is here
   and not at college,
   or with my parents or housemates.
(Although we must remember that 'all I have'
   is an extremely loose term
   encompassing a lot of junk
   that most normal, sane people
   would relegate to the world of garbage.)

This is serious independence
    with a capital 'OHHHH DEAR!'
And I rather like it!

Lord,
    as I sit here,
    letting the evening creep up on me,
    and watch my first sunset
    from my own garden,
    I thank you.

I thank you for all of this.
Watch with me, Lord.

Amen.

THE WORST NEVER HAPPENS

My life, Lord, is
  (or seems to be)
  full of waiting for the worst to happen.
Expecting that, against all the odds
  (even if everything is going well),
  the worst outcome
  will be the only outcome.

It doesn't make much sense really.
I allow my days to be ruled by things that might happen
  rather than by the good things
  which will be there too.

It isn't much fun really.
Everything I do is shadowed
  by this overwhelming fear
  that something bad
  will soon enough put an end to it.

It takes away the fun,
  the enjoyment.
It even manages to wriggle
  into my dreams and ambitions
  and make them seem a waste of time too.
I start to question everything I do
  because I know it'll all go wrong.
And then I let these things get on top of me.

I sit there doing nothing because
  if I do something,
  then it'll go wrong anyway,
  so what's the point?

Yet,
    when something does go right
    I don't appreciate it
    because I am waiting for something else
    to collapse around me!

But what happens when something does go wrong?
Do I live in agony for ever?
Does my life end?
No.
Life goes on.
I cope.
And another day dawns anew.

My fear is so often irrational
    that I forget the support I have around me:
    my friends,
    my family,
    you.

So here I am, Lord,
    at your feet, asking for your help.
As this days dawns and I begin to face
    the good and the bad,
    help me understand
    that even if the worst should happen
    you'll be there with me.

Amen.

SO MUCH TO DO

Today, Lord,
    I already feel snowed under.
My mind is racing and I feel swamped
    by the long list of things I have to do.
I watch as the clock slowly but surely
    sings its silent tune of time passing.
And as I sit and wonder how I'll cope,
    I come to you, Lord.

This list of things is always there.
You think that you've cracked it
    and suddenly there is another bunch of stuff
    which needs to be done.

I get so flustered
    that I waste most of my time
    thinking that I won't be able to do it all
    because there is so much to do,
    or I sit and panic about which to do first.

Some things are more important than others;
    a few are personal
    and a couple are just everyday jobs
    (I hate ironing, Lord).
And the rest are to do with work.
In this busy state of mind so much gets shut out.
So much which is of equal importance
    is pushed to the back of my mind.

It seems selfish,
    but there is no other way through it.
The work needs to be done.
It needs my full attention
    and that's what I give it.

So I begin to forget the other little things
    which aren't on the list of
    'Things to do'.
Things that do not fit in with work,
    or odd jobs,
    but are still essential.

I neglect these little jobs
    because the others are so 'important'.
I do not give time to these minor jobs
    because I am too busy.
I have things to do.
Things that need one hundred per cent of my time.

And amongst the rush and the hurry,
    the deadlines and attainment targets,
    these little things fall to the side.

And I suffer . . .

As I forget to ring someone
    who needs some support.
As I avoid putting pen to paper
    to ask how a friend is doing.
As I get so swept up
    in my own busy little world
    that my real world,
    the world of love,
    of friendship,
    of you . . .

    fades a little.

Lord,
    help me when things get on top of me,
    when the work gets too much
    and the pressures build up.

So that,
    amongst all the 'really important' jobs,
    the lists,
    the piles of paper,
    the demands on my time,
    I'm never too busy to be me.

Amen.

EARLY MORNING IRONING

It's seven in the morning,
   the coffee is on,
   I'm half asleep.
I'm scared,
   and I'm ironing a shirt.

Lord,
   do you have to do this?
Have you ever had to do this?
You see, I don't mind doing it now and again,
   for a special occasion,
   or if I'm out to impress.
But every day?
Every single bloomin' day?

I want my mum.

She has this amazing ability
   to iron a shirt,
   bake bread
   and talk at the same time.
And it only takes her a couple of minutes.
Me?
Well, I've managed to whittle the time
   to a mere twelve minutes.
And that includes the collar!

Oh, Lord,
   this is so adult, it's scary.
I do still want a career,
   go up the ladder,
   earn loads of cash.
(Get married and have children?)

But just lately
   I dream of relaxing in my new house writing books
   and the idea of moving up the career ladder
   seems alien.
Am I the only one who sometimes feels like this, Lord?
I don't know, I really don't.

That's my shirt done, Lord.
I suppose I had better go and put it on,
   tie a 'tie',
   get in my car
   and make my way to the office.

This is suddenly all very strange,
   very alien.
I know I have to do it
   and I know that I *do actually* want to do it.
But deep down, Lord,
   something is missing.

Help me find it, Lord.

Amen.

A WISH TO HEAR

Lord,
   this is a thought
   that has been running around in my mind
   for far too long now,
   and I just want to sit
   and concentrate
   on this one issue
   which I was convinced wasn't a problem.

You see, Lord,
   living on your own is great.
I love it!
I can do what I want
   when I want
   how I want.

If I fancy leaving my pants on the floor
   I will!
If I want to go to the loo with the door open
   I will!
If I want to spend the evening in
   with a video, a bottle of wine
   and a large bag of *Kettle* chips
   I will!

And it's great!

No one to burst in on me!
No one to disapprove!
No one to share it with . . .
And here, Lord,
   is the issue I never previously considered –
   the issue of companionship.

I'm not talking friendship, Lord, or mates.
I'm not thinking of laughs and being daft.

What I'm talking about, Lord,
   is something I see so many have –
   something that frightens me so much
   yet the fear is always tinged
   with slight curiosity.

Most of the time being on my own is great.
I love having the opportunity to be just me.
But occasionally
   (and it gets more and more frequent)
   I would like to have someone by me
   to share all this with.
Someone to hold.

Someone who knew me as I was.
Someone who loved me for all that I am
   and even more
   for all that I'm not.

Someone who didn't get mad
   if I was a little grumpy after work,
   or if I left the toilet seat up now and again.

Someone to whom I could give all that I am,
   all that I will be,
   and share it.

Lord,
   you know me better than all the rest.
I'm not asking for anything
   other than your comfort.

So that,
    when I sit in my chair and wish to hear
    someone call my name from upstairs,
    I will know that some day
    that voice will be real.

Amen.

COMMON THINGS OF EVERY DAY

Before I open my eyes, Lord,
    and the business of the day overwhelms me;
    before I forget all that is
    and become absorbed by phone calls and faxes;
    before I start to jump
    at the sound of the phone ringing
    and live each hour from my computer,
    I want to remember and appreciate
    the little things, Lord.

The common things of every day.

A day is filled with many parts,
    all running into each other.
But when you look back,
    the big important things often fade a little,
    and the smaller ones shine through.

I want to experience
    every second
    of every minute
    of every hour
    of today.

I don't want anything to drift by unnoticed.
I need to experience,
    to feel,
    to enjoy,
    to love
    the common things of every day.

Do you know what I mean, Lord?
I'm not being selfish by saying 'I want!'
    because . . . for once
    I would like to have a day that is not full
    of me being too busy to notice,
    too rushed to care;
    or letting the time I have
    disappear like sand through my fingers.

I would like, Lord,
    to open my eyes this morning and actually see,
    just for once,
    the crazy paving of frost on my window,
    glistening in the early 'good morning' sun.

Do you see, Lord?
Every morning I wake up and become a robot.
A slave to a day run by people I don't really know.

Wash,
    eat,
    work,
    sleep.

Every day it happens,
    and I let it.

But not today.

I am going to get up,
    out of this bed,
    and squeeze every drop of juice
    from every moment of today.
Nothing will pass me by without notice.

I will feel the warmth of my dressing gown
   (which has been left on the radiator)
   as I put it on
   to block out the morning chill.
The sound of the shower
   and the smell of the soap
   will, for once, be important
   as I become awake to the day ahead.

Fresh clean clothes against a fresh clean skin.
The cheerful 'chink' of milk bottles
   at the door.
The taste of the air as I open the door
   and walk on dew-wet grass
   to let the dogs out for their breakfast.
Early morning radio.
The kettle whistling
   to let me know it's ready
   to be poured into the tea pot.

Toast,
   newspapers,
   shoe polish,
   even the sensation of razor
   against stubbly chin.

Do you think I am being over the top, Lord?
Taking things a little too far?
(Not that I've ever done that before!)
It's just that the things I ignore every day –
   things which,
   when given only the time of thought –
   have something to offer,
   something to delight and surprise.

Something to show me
    that amongst all the pressures,
    all the worries,
    all the rushing and hurriedness of my life,
    there is always time
    for the common things of every day.

Amen.

EXPECTATIONS

Lord,
   what do you expect from me?
It's not a daft question, really.
I'd just like to know.
Because I have a feeling
   that now I'm in employment
   people expect certain things of me:
   what I should do,
   how I should act,
   how I should look.
It is all a little different
   to what I'm used to.

Expectations are strange, Lord.
Things that people think I should do,
   or say, or believe
   or whatever.

They are things which to a greater or lesser extent
   predetermine everything that I do.
I'm not saying that they control me,
   just that if people are looking at me
   and don't like what they see,
   then I am obviously not living up
   to their expectations.

But then, Lord,
   whose expectations am I supposed to live up to?
They come from all quarters –
   family,
   friends,
   work.

And in all these situations
   different expectations are placed upon me
   and I change accordingly.

And it is this, Lord,
   that is making me unhappy.
The expectations are all so different,
   and I end up getting it all mixed up,
   and ultimately find
   that I am living up
   to very few of the expectations
   placed upon me.

And what about the expectations I place upon myself?
Lord, I don't even know where to start,
   or if there is any point.
I am so mixed up with this
   that even my own expectations
   seem to lie unfulfilled.

And this leads me to you, Lord.
I'm not perfect.
I am simply someone,
   nothing more,
   nothing less.
No more special than the next, but equal.

Equal in you.

It is your expectations that I wish to fulfil, Lord,
   but I can't.
I try,
   like I try with all the rest,
   yet I still fall down.

But the difference is
    that when I fall down
    you kneel down beside me,
    lift my face to yours and smile.

Lord,
    as I try to live up to so much,
    as I go through changes
    and adjust to this new life,
    remind me
    that the only expectation
    you have of me
    is to love you with all that I am:
    my ups and my downs,
    my successes and failures,
    and the rest that makes me the person you love –
    the person you expect me to be.

Amen.

IN CREDIT!

Lord,
   I know this may not be
   a particularly interesting thing
   for you to witness.
In fact,
   I am quite sure that this next act
   is incredibly common.
But even so,
   I would like you to stand by me
   as I take this magic piece of plastic
   and put it in to the bank machine.

Now when these things used to speak to me
   all I'd see flash by on the screen
   would be a sarcastic computer message
   telling me that I had no money.
Now I am back for revenge.

Ha! Ha!
See, Mr Under-Confident Bank Manager?
I'm in credit – I have money!
I have cash!
I have capital!
I have spending power!
Victory is mine!

For five seconds anyway.

I swear I can hear that machine laughing back at me.
   'You still have a student loan!
   You have a bank loan!
   You have a mortgage to pay off!

You have a car to run!
You have bills to pay!'
So here I am,
    in a position to earn
    just so that I can give it all to someone else.

Everything would be great
    if I was earning what some lucky graduates get.
Do you know, Lord,
    that some people leave college
    and get a job that pays over £20,000 a year?
How is that possible?
That is a whole £17,000 more than me.
(Well, not quite: I am prone to exaggeration.)

I sound a little bitter, don't I?
I'm not really,
    I'm just being a little ungracious and greedy.
(Perhaps not greedy – not much anyway.)

I am so impatient.

I forget how lucky I am.
At least I have a job.
At least I have prospects
    (though my lovely boss would probably
    like to disagree for the fun of it).
And I am happy.

Lord,
    as I look and see my money flash by on the screen,
    as I get in to my car,
    drive to my house,
    or get ready for work,
    I begin to realise how insignificant money really is.

Thinking about it,
   if I had £20,000 a year
   I'd spend it just as fast.
Justifying buying an even faster car
   would not be a problem.
New clothes would present very little difficulty
   and a crazy social life would be a must.

So perhaps, Lord,
   starting were I am
   will teach me a little more
   than being given it all on a plate.

A little humble pie now,
   and maybe I won't be so hungry
   further down the road.

Amen.

SOMETHING IS HAPPENING

Lord,
   I'm at work
   and I have a problem;
   (why I told you that I don't know,
   as you probably knew already).

Well, sort of.

You see,
   I've been here some time now,
   and I have to say that at no point was I ever sure
   that what I was doing was right,
   or that I would ever get any results.

Until now.

I have in front of me the morning post.
To he honest,
   it would be very easy indeed
   to persuade myself that none of this is mine,
   and that if it is,
   it is merely all the junk mail
   that never made it to my previous addresses.

It is a mountain of huge jiffy bags,
   a pile of envelopes –
   all the trappings of someone who stays at home
   and writes books.

What do I do with it all?
Who are these people writing to me?
What do I do once the stuff is opened?

And why do I have the distinct impression
   that once again
   you are sitting back with a huge smug grin,
   trying not to laugh?

You knew, didn't you?
In fact, you've known all along!
Why couldn't you have told me?

What would have been the damage
   to let on about this one evening
   with one of those visions or angel visitations
   (I've always wondered what they look like)
   or a sign?

After all those screaming sessions;
   the thousands of times I've gone crazy
   not knowing where I was going
   or why I was here;
   the yells of despair
   as I demanded that you tell me;
   the tears that fell during all that confusion.

Years I have spent
   not knowing what I was doing
   or where I was going.
I never knew what was around the corner.
I never had a thought about my future other than
   'Well, it'll be interesting to see where I am in
   about five years' time.'

Well,
   I'm here now
   and you never told me.
Ever.

Why?

Would it really have altered my life?
Would the change really have been that
   significant?

The answer is yes,
   isn't it?

Lord,
   you know me too well
   (I know that it's all part of the job,
   but it's still amazing).
If I had known that this was going to happen,
   if I had known for absolute certain
      that everything was going to be all right,
   I'd have slackened off.
I'm not talking academically here,
   as I need no excuse there for a little slacking.

I'm talking emotionally,
   mentally,
   spiritually.

I wouldn't have cared so passionately
   about what I now have,
   and where I am at,
   or where I'm going.
The experiences of these last few years
   would not have caused me so much pain
   or taught me so much:
      I wouldn't have cared so much about the fact
      that I thought I was being destroyed.

The truth of the matter was
   that I was just going through a painful birth.
Born of fire, almost.

Without the ups and downs,
   the good and the bad,
   the confusion, questioning
   and searching
   of these years
   I wouldn't be here now.

So it only leaves me, Lord,
   with one option.
I must thank you,
   but for something I never thought
   I would thank you for.
And it is only you who will understand.
It is only you who truly know
   what I mean when I say,
   'My Lord, thank you for the pain.'

Amen.